The Drum Bl

A collection of snare drum exercises and tips to improve snare drum performance.

By **Jeremie Foster**

Copyright © 2022 Jeremie Foster

All rights reserved. This book or parts thereof may not be reproduced in any form, stored in any retrieval system, or transmitted in any form by any means—electronic, mechanical, photocopy, recording, or otherwise—without prior written permission of the publisher, except as provided by United States of America copyright law. For permission requests, write to the author, at:

Jeremie Foster
jeremiefoster@gmail.com

This publication is dedicated to my loving mother, courageous sister, and beautiful God-fearing wife.

TABLE OF CONTENTS

vi	Table of Contents
viii	Preface
x	Introduction
1	Foundation: The Grips
5	The Accent-Tap Blueprints
15	The Double-Stop Blueprints
23	The Timing Blueprints
31	The Diddle Blueprints

TABLE OF CONTENTS

43   The Double-Beat Blueprints

51   The Flam Blueprints

61   The Paradiddle Blueprints

71   40 Essential Rudiments Blueprint

75   Bonus: Jeremie's Favorites

89   Glossary

103   About The Author

Preface

God is good. I never imagined myself writing a book, not even a book for drummers. So for this and everything I have, I give God all the glory.

The state of percussion in the world today is nothing less than amazing. Every day, I see kids and adults of all ages finding new ways to implement the art of percussion in their everyday lives. Seeing this makes me smile every time. It makes me eager to want to help those individuals become more in tune with the passion for percussion that resides within them. I want to help them get the resources they need to become an even better percussionist so that they can have much more of an impact on this Earth in the area of percussion.

I remember being a kid in middle school, and all I could think about every day was the next rudiment I would learn and how I would play it all day. I remember how driven I was then and how hopeful I was to get better at my craft. I would spend hours and hours listening to music and drumming on a pillow to perfect my rudimental skills. I remember vividly how excited I would get to talk about percussion with my family, friends, and loved ones. I remember that fire I had at such a young age for the art of percussion, and that fire is what I want to ignite into everyone who reads this book.

If you've never picked up a drumstick, it's never too late to start. No drummer ever was amazing at drumming the first time they picked up a pair of drumsticks. You have the spark, which is why you picked up this book; now it's time to set that fire ablaze and learn all you can. In addition to whatever personal lessons or music/band classes you take, this book will be that extra push to becoming an elite drummer.

If you have experience with drumming, there is no limit to how much knowledge you should gain in your craft. I find it very intriguing to discover things about drum performance that I did not know before. It's as if I feel my brain expand while learning to play a new type of grid, hybrid rudiment, snare solo, stick trick, etc. As gifted as you are, continue to be a student as you read this book, and you will be even more successful in your drumming career.

Introduction

If you're reading this, that means you are interested in obtaining and learning the 'blueprint' to drum performance. You've come to the right place.

When I first started playing drums, I did not practice with a metronome only because I did not own one. I actually didn't know what a metronome was until middle school (mid-2000s). At that time, metronome apps on the phone weren't a thing, and I couldn't afford a physical metronome. Instead, I practiced while listening to music and letting the music be the tempo marker for me as I practiced. I want every reader of this exercise book to have the same feeling I had when drumming to music. So to ensure that, I placed scannable QR codes in every piece of sheet music that will direct you to various hip-hop instrumentals, so you can listen to a cool beat as you play through each exercise.

When it comes to the exercises themselves, if you are a beginner, start slowly as you learn each piece. The more you practice at a moderately slow tempo, the better you genuinely understand how the rhythms are placed and played. As you get more acquainted with the exercises, you can start incorporating the hip-hop instrumental to play along with!

For the more advanced percussionists, there is not one exercise in this book that is less important than the other. With that being said, It is still vital that you practice even the 'easiest' of exercises to truly benefit from what the exercise targets, whether it be proper form, stick control, diddle interpretation, or accent-tap. Everyone can chop, but understanding the fundamentals separates the elite drummers from the rest.

FOUNDATION: THE GRIPS

"Life is not what we drum up for God, but what He drums up in us."
— Gary Custis

The Grips: Tradition Grip vs. Matched Grip

One of the first concepts to grasp in snare drum performance before even learning music is how a drumstick should be held appropriately while performing. Two types of grips are commonly used in snare drum performance: *traditional grip* and *matched grip*. Review the following sections of each grip, and ensure the desired grip form is fully understood. Remember: proper grip produces proper beats, thus resulting in excellent snare drum performance.

The Traditional Grip

The **traditional grip**, less commonly referred to as the *orthodox* or *jazz grip*, is one of the more common forms of grips used by drumline organizations and percussion ensembles worldwide. In this method of gripping, the way the stick is held is different for both hands. See below for a front view of the traditional grip.

On the left hand, the stick is held in an *underhand* position, with the lower-mid end placed on the cusp between the thumb and index finger; and the upper-mid end between the middle and ring finger, with the stick resting on the ring finger. The thumb and index finger are to touch, fully wrapping around the stick and the middle finger curls over the stick in the same fashion as the index finger. As the stick rests on the ring finger, the ring finger is curled under, alongside a curled pinky finger. See below for an image of the left hand:

On the right hand, the stick is held in an *overhand* position, where the stick is grasped fully, allowing all fingers to wrap around the stick, with the thumb placed on the side. The edges of the thumb and index fingers are to touch to ensure stick security. The right hand should be parallel to the drumhead, specifically the *German grip*, which is the most used way of holding the right-hand stick within drumline organizations. See below for an above and below view of the right hand:

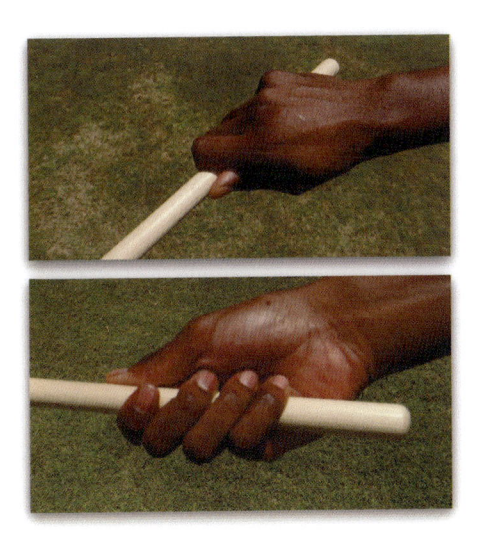

The Matched Grip

The **matched grip** is the lesser form of grip used within drumline organizations; however widely popular among percussion ensembles and drum set performers. The term *matched* refers to how the stick is held on the left hand, matching how the stick is held on the right hand. They both share the *overhand* form used by the right hand of the traditional grip, thus having the left hand and right hand become an exact mirror of each other. Both hands should be parallel to the drumhead, or using the *German grip* on both hands. See below for an example of how the matched grip should be displayed:

THE ACCENT-TAP BLUEPRINTS

"When you approach this instrument for the first time, what comes out of you is simply what you feel."
— Dennis Chambers

The Accent-Tap Exercise

Accent tap exercises are vital in developing overall stick control. An **accent** is a note played with emphasis and is denoted by a symbol called an **accent mark**, a notation similar to the 'greater than' symbol, which is usually placed either on top or below the note. Exercises with an Accent-Tap baseline focus on controlling accents, compared to controlling taps, and the overall timing when playing the two together.

To understand an accent is to understand how a stroke is played. There are four types of strokes in snare drum performance: **a full stroke, a down stroke, a tap stroke,** and **an up stroke.**

The Full Stroke (Start: Up; End: Up)
The **full stroke** is the more basic, general stroke. It is required when playing sheet music with dynamic markings of mezzo-forte to fortissimo and beyond. With full strokes, the stick starts in an up position and ends in an up position after the drum is stricken. When the stick comes back up after hitting the drum, or when the stick **rebounds**, the rebound of the stick should be controlled, allowing the hand to follow the natural motion of the stick back to the up position.

The Down Stroke (Start: Up; End: Down)
The **down stroke** is a stroke that is accented. The stick height for this type of stroke starts in an up position; however, it ends in a down position, with the stick hovering slightly over the drum. When this type of stroke is played, the back fingers should be closed during the strike to have a more closed grip at the down position.

The Tap Stroke (Start: Down; End: Down)
Tap strokes are full strokes that are played at a lower dynamic. The stroke starts at a low stick height and ends at a low stick height. Tap strokes usually require only the wrist due to the lack of motion used, but it may vary depending on the music's requirements.

The Up Stroke (Start: Down; End: Up)
The only purpose of the **up stroke** is to prepare the hand for the subsequent strokes. The main trick to these strokes is that the stick's rebound must be enhanced with the hand's grip to assist the stick in reaching the up position. This grip may include using the wrist and fingers, contingent on the upcoming stroke.

Usually consisting of complete wrist extended accents and 3-inch taps, working on accent-tap exercises is one of the most important things you can do to build excellent sound quality fundamentally when practiced correctly.

The following is a basic example of an accent-tap exercise:

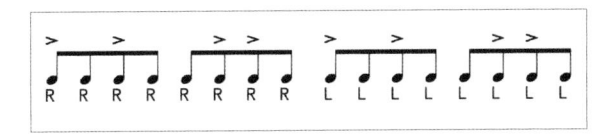

When playing the accent, despite playing with emphasis, try not to overplay the accent. Overplaying an accent can cause a distorted sound and force subsequent tap sounds to be much lighter and less controlled, which could be a huge issue when adding more things like flams, diddles, and rolls, placed on top of those taps.

As you begin to read through each exercise within the *Accent-Tap Blueprints*, keep in mind that a good, well-balanced accent, when compared to the tap, is what we are looking for.

When you start to get comfortable with each exercise and decide to add some speed, pay close attention and ensure that the taps, or inner beats, remain relaxed. Playing at a faster tempo can easily cause the taps to be played at a higher height, but keep in mind that doing so would hinder the sound quality and create an uncontrolled percussion performance. Enjoy!

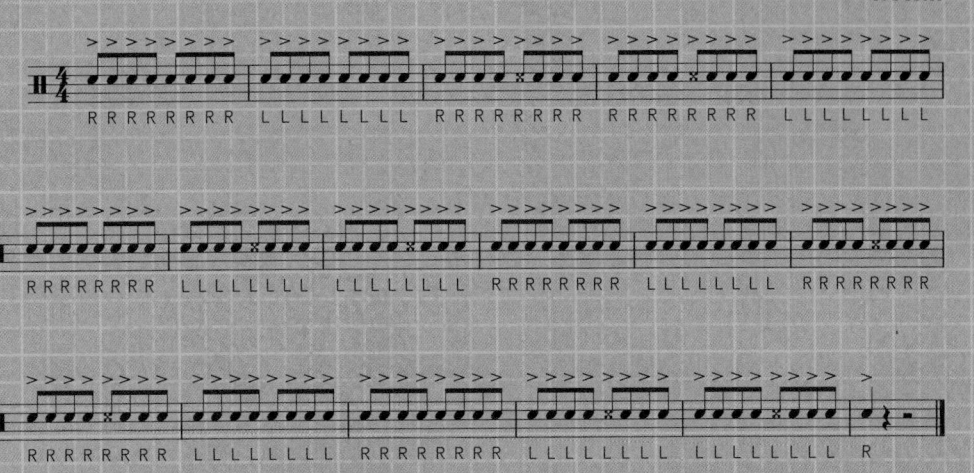

Blueprint #1

J. Foster

Blueprint #2

J. Foster

Blueprint #3

J. Foster

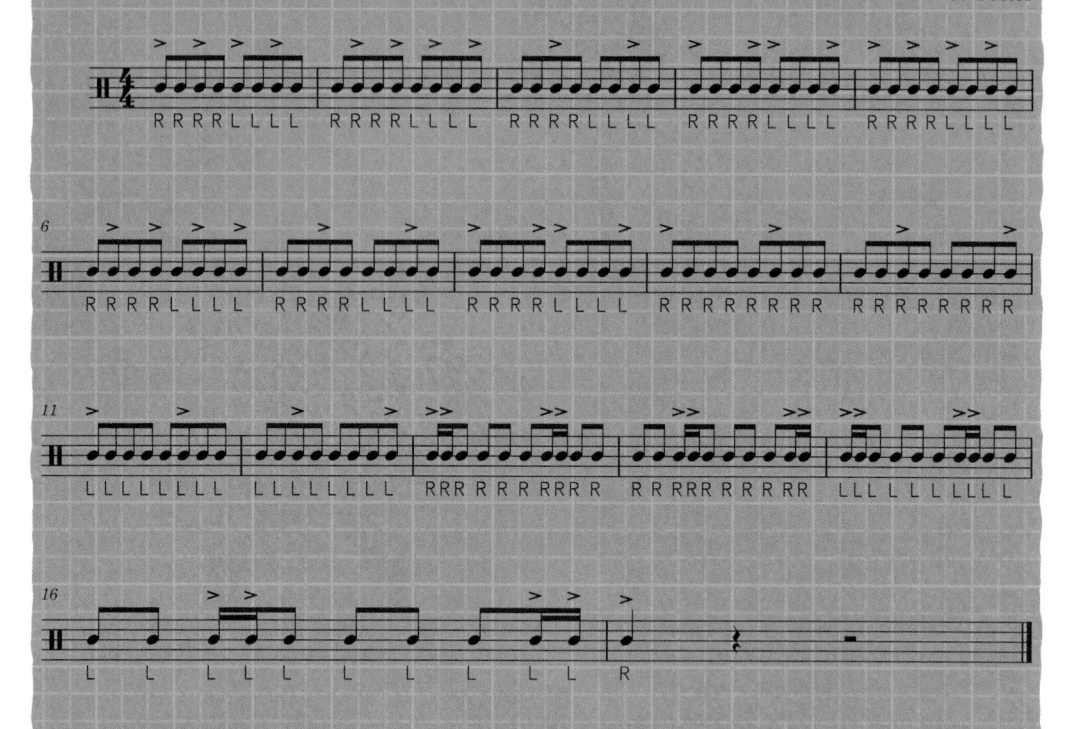

Blueprint #4

J. Foster

Notes

THE DOUBLE-STOP BLUEPRINTS

"Playing fast on the drums is one thing. But to play music, to play with people for others to listen to, that's something else. That's a whole other world."
— Tony Williams

The Double-Stop Exercise

Double-stop exercises are very helpful in developing dexterity and strength in the weak hand of a percussionist. A **double-stop** is a note played by striking the drum with both hands at once, creating a flat-sounding note called a **flat flam**. A double-stop, or flat flam, is typically notated by having one stem with two note heads and the letter *B* written under it as the *sticking* to indicate the use of both hands to play the note.

An example of a typical double-stop exercise can be found below:

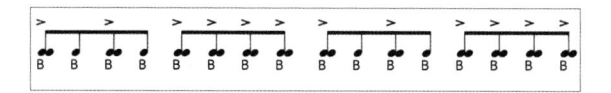

Like accent-tap exercises, double-stop exercises emphasize the controlling of accents and taps with both hands simultaneously. These exercises are essential due to the constant need to strengthen the weaker hand.

When executing a double-stop exercise, remember that equal intensity is to be used on both hands for every stroke of the flat flam. Whether the flat-flam is to be played at a low height as an inner beat or at a high height as an accent, both hands must have the same stroking power to receive the proper sound and develop the desired wrist strength.

As you go through each exercise within the *Double-Stop Blueprints,* remember that the key to playing clean double-stops is matching the technique, stick height, and velocity with both hands. Always remember: If both hands can't play in unison perfectly, then both hands will not be able to alternate evenly either. Enjoy!

Blueprint #5

J. Foster

Blueprint #6

J. Foster

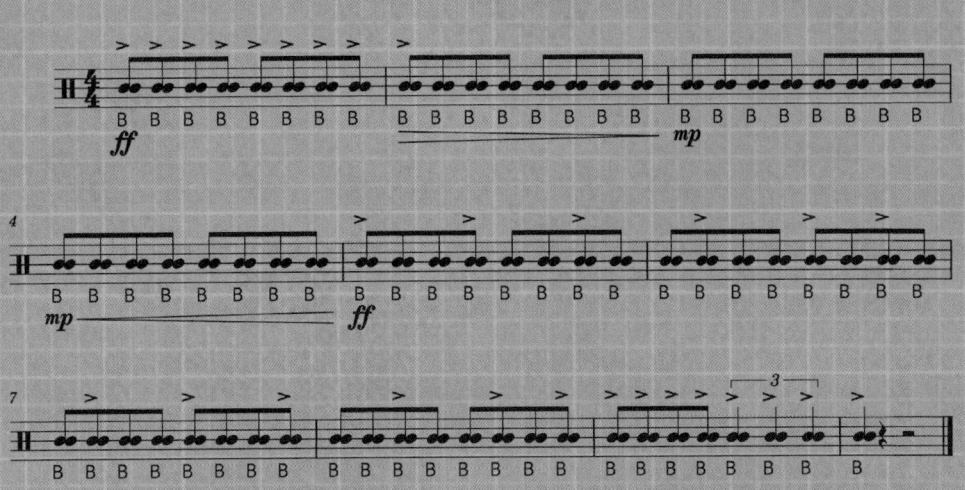

Blueprint #7

J. Foster

Blueprint #8

J. Foster

Notes

THE TIMING BLUEPRINTS

"You only get better by playing."
— Buddy Rich

The Timing Exercise

Timing exercises are incredibly vital, as they help improve the timing in which rhythms are played during performance. One common issue that drummers have is their timing and note spacing. It is important to note that 'timing' is not the same as 'time keeping,' though they are often confused. **Timekeeping** refers to a drummer's ability to play in time with the pulse of the music. Whereas **timing** refers to a drummer's coordination of his/her limbs and their playing relative to the beat or rest of the band.

Understanding timing is easy. It's all about understanding the **pulse**, or beat, of which the exercise/cadence is being played. For example, feel your heartbeat. At this moment, your heart rate should be at a steady tempo. Now copy your heartbeat's rhythm by clasping your index finger and thumb together simultaneously with your heartbeat. Are you able to stay on that steady tempo? Okay, now this time, instead of copying every beat of your heart rate, skip the 3rd beat, to where it is 1…2…(rest)…..4. Did you stay on tempo that time? Were you able to play that 4th beat in time after the rest? If so, good job! If not, it is okay, as all it takes is a few repetitions of *The Timing Blueprints,* and your understanding of note spacing will be impeccable!

An example of how timing exercises are usually written out can be seen as follows:

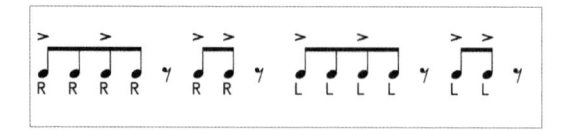

As you can see, timing exercises can be pretty straightforward; however, they serve just as much importance as the previous exercises. Keep in mind that most of the exercises within *The Timing Blueprints* chapter are simple, but pay close attention to the pulse of each exercise so that each note can be played in time. There will be exercises that have several 8th note **rests** back-to-back, but make sure to maintain the tempo to ensure accurate note space between each note. Improper note spacing can destroy a snare drum performance, individually and within a Drumline, so it's best to pay close attention to that aspect. Enjoy!

Blueprint #9

J. Foster

Blueprint #10

J. Foster

Blueprint #11

J. Foster

Blueprint #12

J. Foster

Notes

THE DIDDLE BLUEPRINTS

"Put the work in, then put it out to the world! You're more than ready."

– Ralph Nader

The Diddle Exercise

Implementing diddle exercises in personal practice is the key to achieving elite diddle interpretation during snare drum performance. A **diddle** is a note consisting of two consecutively played strokes on one hand. Diddles are typically notated by having one or several slashes on a single note, depending on the type of diddle-rudiment the music asks for.

There are instances when the space between the two notes of the diddle can be too far, causing a more open, swung diddle, thus hindering the rest of the snare piece. Likewise, a diddle's note spacing can be too short during performance, causing a more buzz-sounding, uncontrolled diddle. Diddle exercises can help achieve that perfect diddle, one that is played at the appropriate time within the snare piece.

A typical diddle exercise can be seen below:

Diddle Interpretation

Diddle interpretation refers to the clarity and cleanliness of a diddle that is being played. Because diddles are so crucial in snare drum performance, in this book, we have broken the diddle down into three groups, which are different based on the technique required to play them: **the double stroke, the 'low-key' diddle, and the diddle**. This is because, as the tempo increases or decreases, it ultimately changes the approach of how the two diddles should be played.

The Double Stroke (0 to 120 BPMs)

The double stroke consists of just that: double strokes or two full strokes. It is purposely titled the 'double stroke' to highlight that when this type of diddle is played, both strokes of the diddle have full control. When these types of diddles are played, the wrist should be the primary fulcrum, and the weight in the hand should be even, using minimal forearm unless deemed necessary from the dynamics involved. Double strokes are usually played at slower tempos, from 0 to 120 BPMs, and are very legato.

The 'Low-key' Diddle (120 to 160 BPMs)

The 'low-key diddle' is the type of diddle that is the middle point between the first and last categories. These types of diddles can be found in faster paradiddles or doubles strokes that are placed over a 16th note pattern. Low-key diddles are usually played at moderate tempos ranging from 120 to 160 BPMs. Remember that fingers should still be used to support the diddle when these types of diddles are played. The forearm is not solely in use for these types of diddles. There should instead be an even use of the forearm and wrist.

The Diddle (160+ BPMs)

The diddle is involved in basically any kind of fast roll exercise in music and can typically be found within pieces that are 160 BPMs and beyond. It is important to note that when performing these types of diddles, now that we are at a faster tempo, the pressure and weight of the hand and stick should be to the front of the fulcrum. However, play calm and relaxed, and try not to squeeze too hard, as it could cause harm to arms and tendons.

Forearm should be used when playing these types of diddles. The forearm help is needed because the arm has much more weight and will help support and put more speed into the motions, which will help the diddles truly speak at that tempo.

As you go through each exercise within *The Diddle Blueprints* and start incorporating the hip-hop instrumentals during practice, keep in mind the above points. Enjoy!

Blueprint #13

J. Foster

Blueprint #14

J. Foster

Blueprint #15

J. Foster

Blueprint #16

J. Foster

Blueprint #17

J. Foster

Blueprint #18

J. Foster

Blueprint #19

J. Foster

Blueprint #20

J. Foster

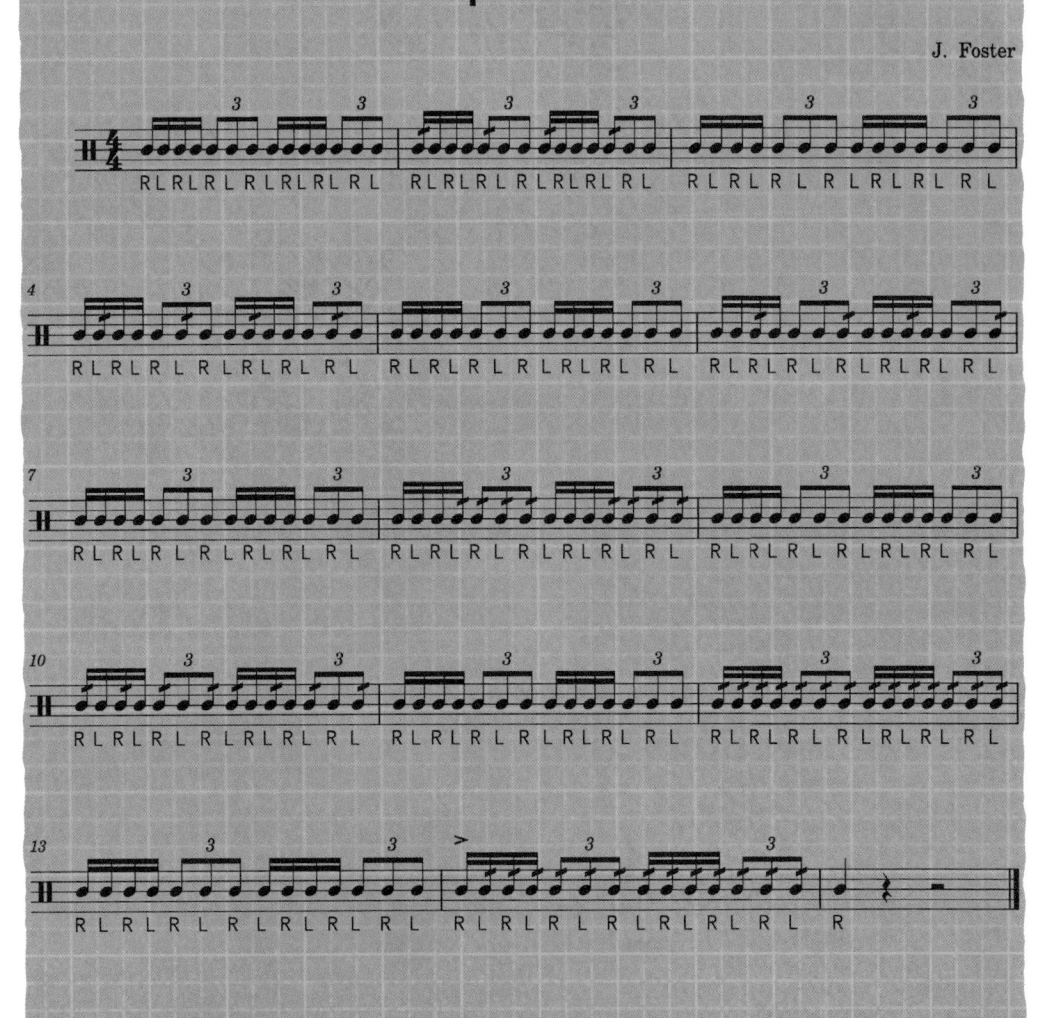

Notes

THE DOUBLE-BEAT BLUEPRINTS

"Practice makes perfect, and even if you think you're perfect, you're not. Keep practicing."
—Eric Moore

The Double-Beat Exercise

Double-beat exercises help improve double and triple strokes and their sound quality during snare drum performance. These exercises are some of the most essential exercises in rudimental drumming, as they are necessary for amazing sounding rolls.

A typical double beat exercise would be written as such:

```
R R  R R  R R  R R  R R  R | L L  L L  L L  L L  L L  L
```

Keep in mind that when playing the strokes in the double-beat exercises within this blueprint, the wrist must direct each stroke with a relaxed and calm rebound. Each note of the double or triple stroke should be even. Try not to have a wrist that is too stiff and tight because it will result in a double/triple stroke that sounds choppy, producing more than the 2/3 notes that the double/triple stroke calls for. Sometimes that can also result in the 1st stroke being much louder than the 2nd or 3rd strokes.

Uniformity between the left and right hands is critical when performing these exercises. Make sure that the sticks move the same way during the performance of these exercises for both hands. The initial note of each double/triple stroke should start with a wrist turn. The second/third notes of each double/triple stroke should still use some wrist action, but they are produced mainly with the fingers for the right hand and thumb and index fingers for the left hand. Then, as the tempo increases, the degree of wrist turn decreases, depending more on the fingers.

As you go through each exercise within the *Double-Beat Blueprints* and start incorporating the play-along track, keep these points in mind, and there will be a clear improvement during snare drum performance. Enjoy!

Blueprint #21

J. Foster

Blueprint #22

J. Foster

Blueprint #23

J. Foster

Blueprint #24

J. Foster

Notes

THE FLAM BLUEPRINTS

"Excellence isn't an act, it's a habit."
— Quincy Jones

The Flam Exercise

Incorporating flam exercises in everyday practice is a great way to improve flam-based rudiments during snare drum performance. A **flam** is comprised of two individual strokes that are executed at two different heights. Their primary purpose is to create a longer and thicker sounding note compared to one single stroke.

Below shows how a flam is written and played:

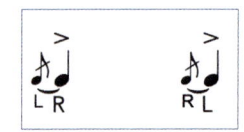

Please take a look at how the flam is written: it consists of a **grace note,** or an extra note added as an embellishment, and an accented note, or a **primary note**. When performing a right-hand flam, the primary note is played by the right hand, with the grace note being played slightly before on the left. The opposite is applied to the left-hand flam: the primary note is on the left hand, with the grace note played slightly before on the right hand. The grace note in this rudiment should be played at a low height, which is only achievable by doing an 'up stroke.' The remaining accented note should start at a much higher height but stop at a low height after striking the drum, which is achievable only by executing a down stroke. Because the difference in stick heights is so vast, the accented note should hit the drum slightly after the grace note is played, which will create that thicker sounding note.

The flam can be a bit complicated to perform with good sound quality. Technically, the grace note can be played as far from the accented note as desired, but to achieve an excellent sound quality of the flam, it is best to play the grace note as close to the primary note as possible but not at the same time. Performing the grace note simultaneously as the primary note will produce what is known as a "flat flam," or a flam similar to a double-stop.

As you go through each exercise within the *Flam Blueprints* and start to incorporate the flam within other flam-based rudiments, keep in mind to keep the grace note as low as possible and avoid playing the grace note at the same time as the primary note. Let's get to drumming!

Blueprint #25

J. Foster

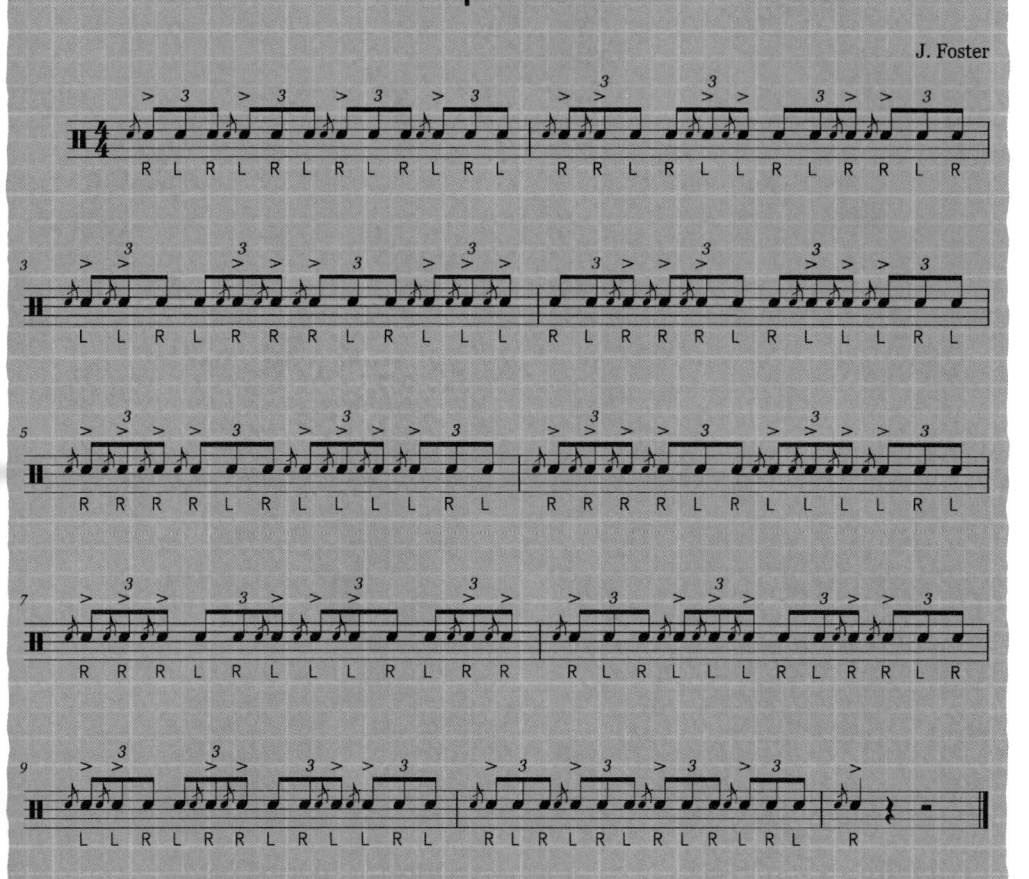

Blueprint #26

J. Foster

Blueprint #27

J. Foster

Blueprint #28

J. Foster

Blueprint #29

J. Foster

Notes

THE PARADIDDLE BLUEPRINTS

"Stamina is the force that drives the drumming; it's not really a sprint."
— Buddy Rich

The Paradiddle Exercise

The **single paradiddle** is one of the most basic rhythmic patterns, or rudiments, that is the building block of many snare performance pieces today. Mastering this drum rudiment opens the doors to several new beats, solos, and snare grooves. Consisting of 2 single strokes and one double stroke, and with the sticking as 'right-left-right-right' or 'left-right-left-left,' the paradiddle is excellent for adding a little complexity to snare performance.

Below shows how a paradiddle is written and played:

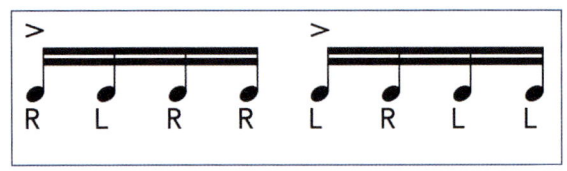

```
>           >
R L R R     L R L L
```

As stated earlier, the paradiddle consists of 2 single strokes and one double stroke, and the same is done on the alternate hand. It can be complicated to have mastery of this rudiment when performed at faster tempos, so be sure to take your time and master the foundations first.

As with every rudiment, it is imperative to understand the proper stick grip required to have an even-sounding paradiddle. If you haven't done so, review *The Accent Tap Blueprints* and *The Diddle Blueprint* chapters to ensure the concepts of playing both single stroke and double stroke rolls are fully grasped.

As you begin to improve on the foundations of paradiddle performance and dive into the exercises within this chapter, keep in mind the kind of stroke, whether a tap or an accent, each note in the rudiment requires. Make sure all unaccented notes are evenly distributed, no matter the practicing tempo. These points will be critical as you progress and start to incorporate the play-a-long music. Enjoy!

Blueprint #30

J. Foster

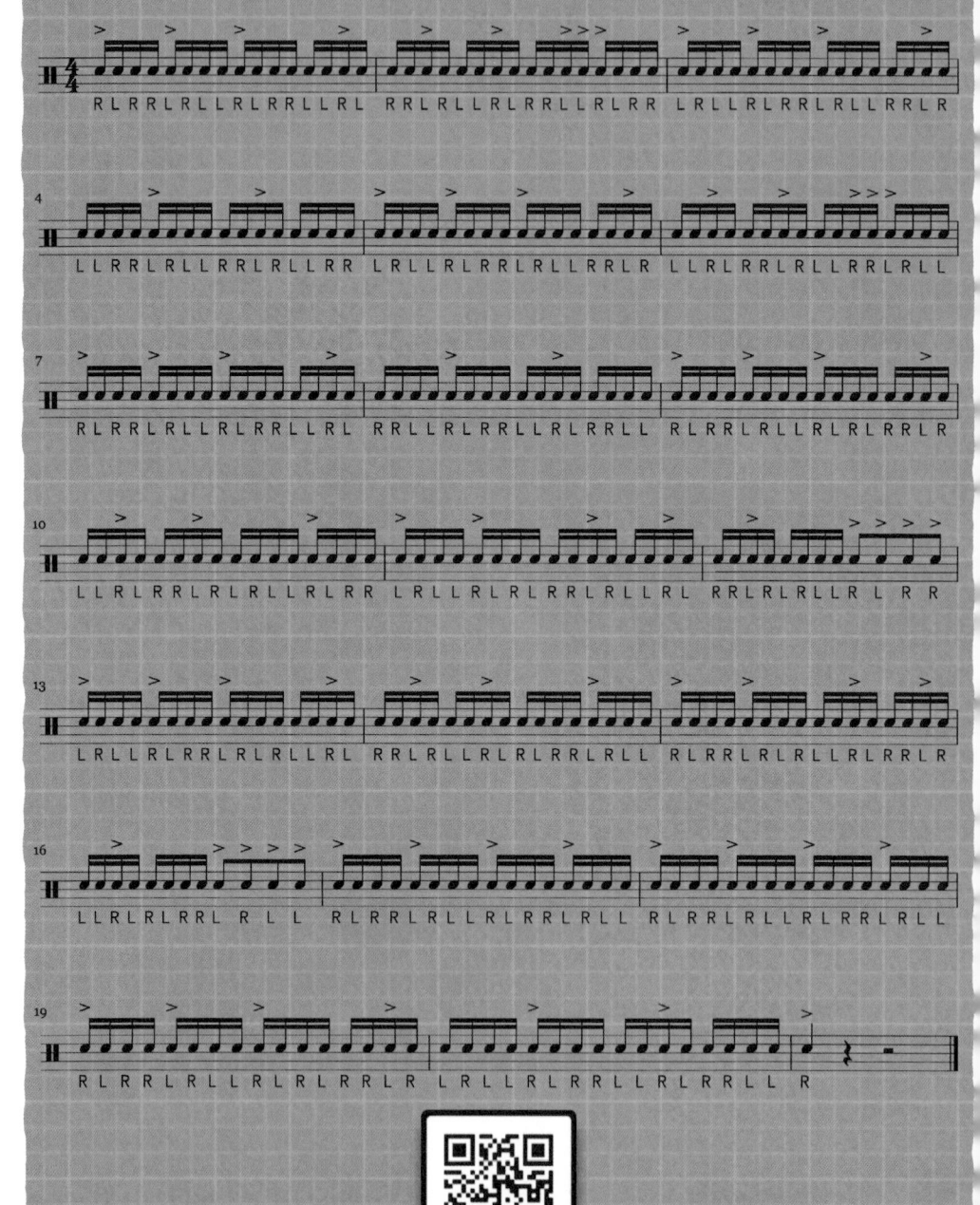

The Paradiddle Blueprints

Blueprint #31

J. Foster

RLRRLRLLRLRRLLRL RRLRLLRLRRLLRLRR LRLLRLRRLRLLRRLR

LLRLRLLRRLRLLRR LRLLRLRRLRLLRRLR LLRLRRLRLLRRLRLL

RLRRLRLLRLRRLLRL RRLLRLRRLLRLRRLL RLRRLRLLRLRLRRLR

LLRLRRLRLRLLRLRR LRLLRLRLRRLRLLRL RRLRLLRLRL R R

LRLLRLRRLRLLRRLRL RRLRLLRLRLRRLRLL RLRRLRLLRLLRRLR

LLRLRLRRL R L L RLRRLRLLRLRRLRLL RLRRLRLLRLRRLRLL

RLRRLRLLRLRLRRLR LRLLRLRRLLRLRRLL R

Blueprint #32

J. Foster

RLRRLRLLRLRRLRLL RLRRLLRLRRLLRRR LRLLRLRRLLRLRR

LRLLRRLRLLRRLRLL RLRRLLRLRRLLRLRR LRLLRRLRLLRRLRLL

RLRRLRLLRLRRLRLL RLRRLRLLRLRRLRLL RLRRLRLLRLRRLRLL

RLRRLRLLRLRRLLRLL R

Blueprint #33

J. Foster

Blueprint #34

J. Foster

Blueprint #35

J. Foster

Notes

40 ESSENTIAL RUDIMENTS BLUEPRINT

"Your talent is God's gift to you. What you do with it is your gift back to God"

– Leo Buscaglia

40 Essential Rudiments Blueprint

Single Stroke Roll

Single Stroke Four

Single Stroke Seven

Multiple Bounce Roll

Triple Stroke Roll

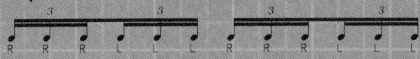

Double Stroke (Open) Roll

Five Stroke Roll

Six Stroke Roll

Seven Stroke Roll

Nine Stroke Roll

Ten Stroke Roll

Eleven Stroke Roll

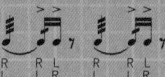

Thirteen Stroke Roll

Fifteen Stroke Roll

Seventeen Stroke Roll

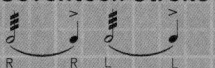

Single Paradiddle

Double Paradiddle

Triple Paradiddle

Single Paradiddle-Diddle

Flam

40 Essential Rudiments Blueprint

Flam Accent

Flam Tap

Flamacue

Flam Paradiddle

Single Flammed Mill

Single Paradiddle-Diddle

Pataflafla

Swiss Army Triplet

Inverted Flam Tap

Flam Drag

Drag

Single Drag Tap

Double Drag Tap

Lesson 25

Single Dragadiddle

Drag Paradiddle #1

Drag Paradiddle #2

Single Ratamacue

Double Ratamacue

Triple Ratamacue

BONUS: JEREMIE'S FAVORITES

"Done practicing for the day? Congrats! Now practice some more."

– Jeremie Foster

Congratulations! You made it through all of the blueprints! I am more than positive that your hands are getting better and better. Spend more time practicing and paying attention to the little details, and you will be an elite snare drummer in no time!

In this section, I decided to put a few of my favorite snare solos, licks, sprees, and advanced warmups from over the years, all written by me, of course! Check them out!

Yahweh's 7 Lick

J. Foster

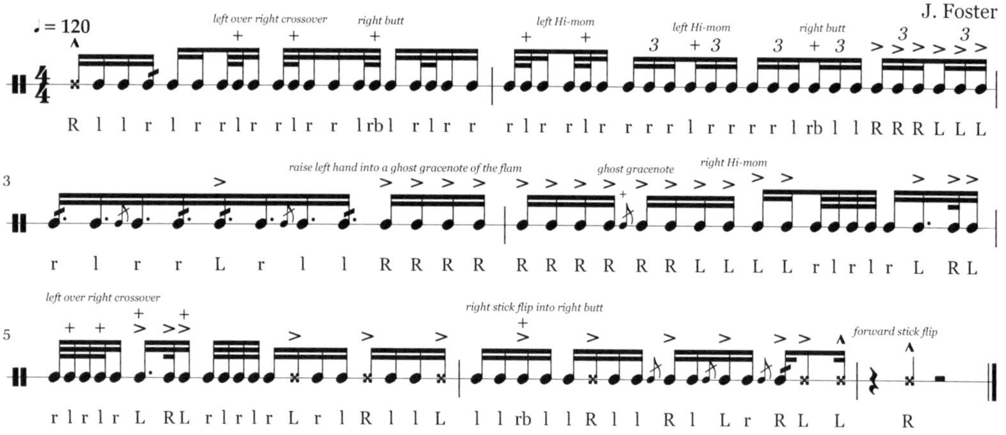

Bonus: Jeremie's Favorites

Add-To-The-Rhythm Exercise

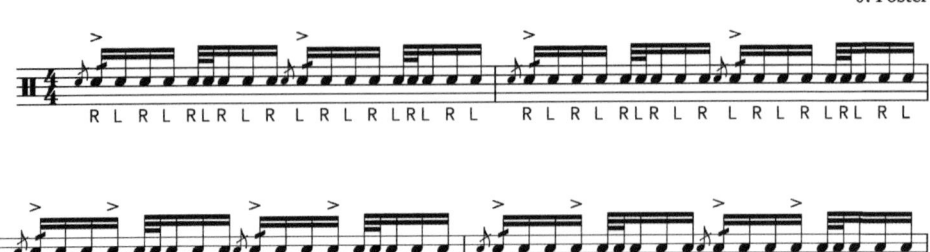

J. Foster

Bonus: Jeremie's Favorites

Resolution Spree

J. Foster

"I'm Closing My Eyes" Snare Cover

BYOS

J. Foster

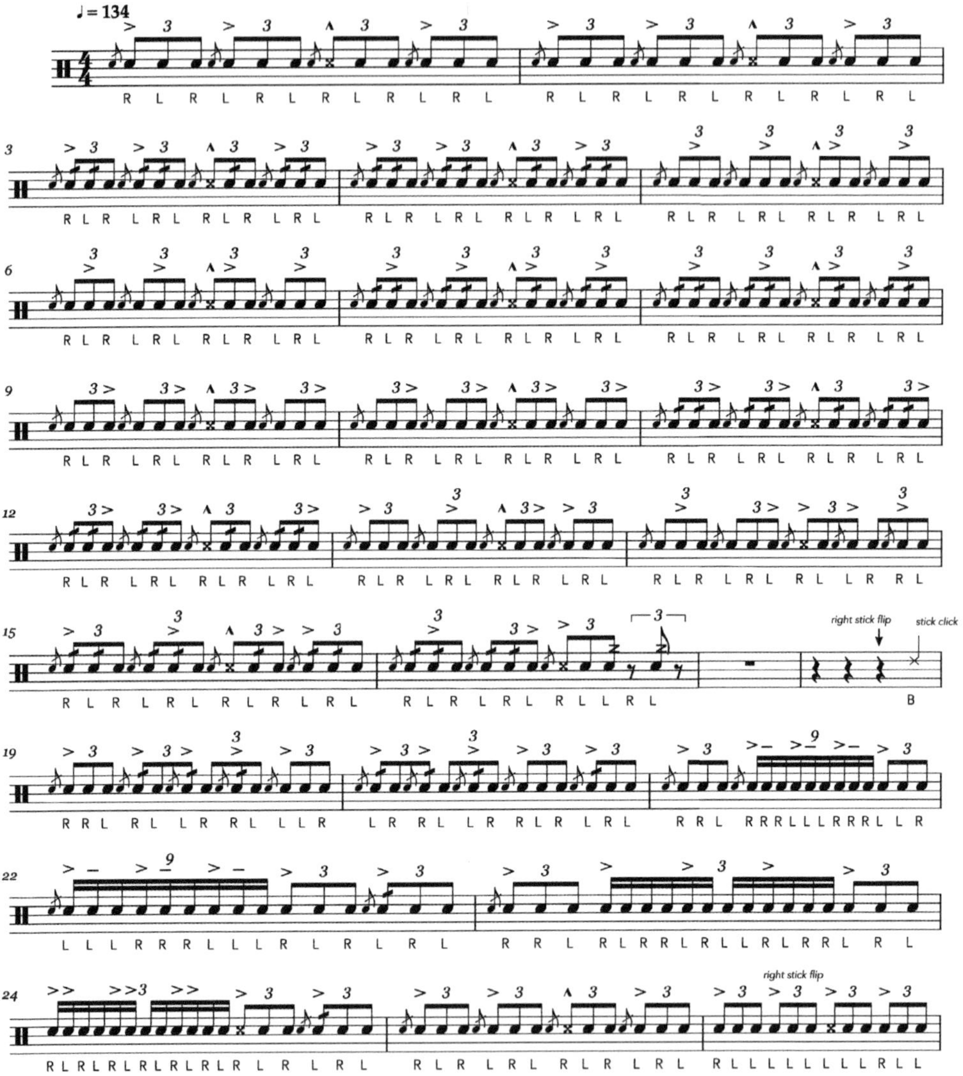

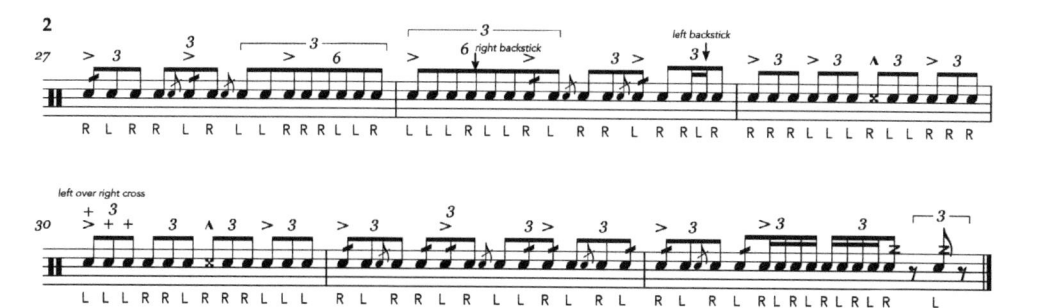

Bonus: Jeremie's Favorites

3-in-4 Exercise

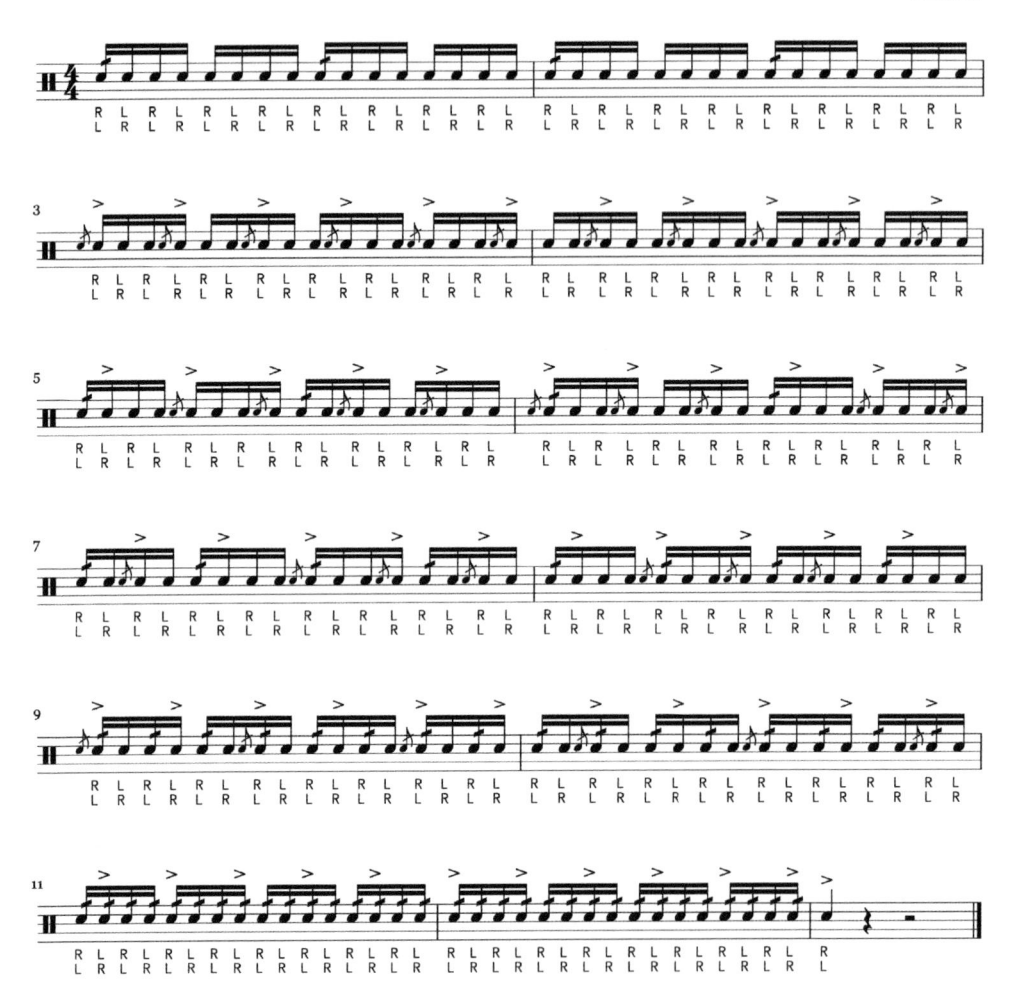

J. Foster

Bonus: Jeremie's Favorites

Office Tingz I

J. Foster

Office Tingz II

J. Foster

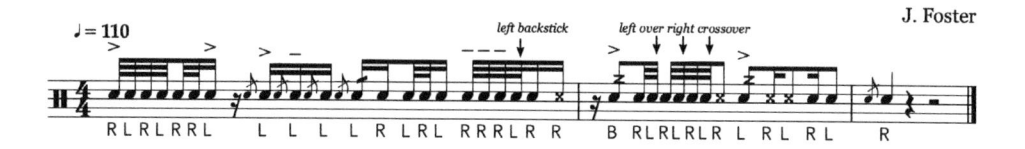

Office Tingz III

J. Foster

Office Tingz IV

J. Foster

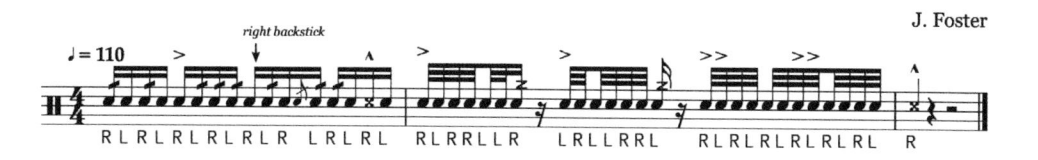

Office Tingz V

J. Foster

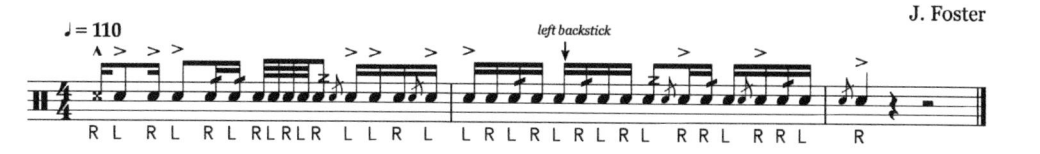

Bonus: Jeremie's Favorites

Midterm Spree

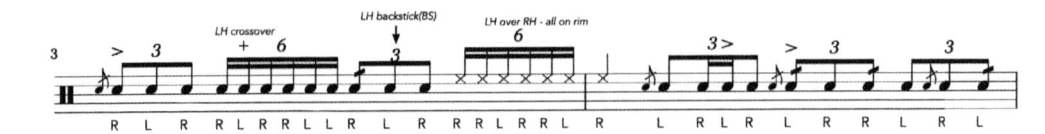

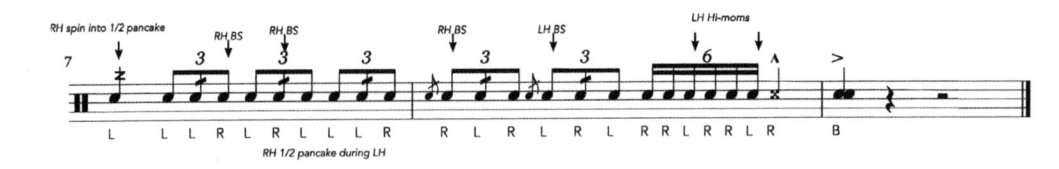

J. Foster

Bonus: Jeremie's Favorites

6 Stroke Single Grid

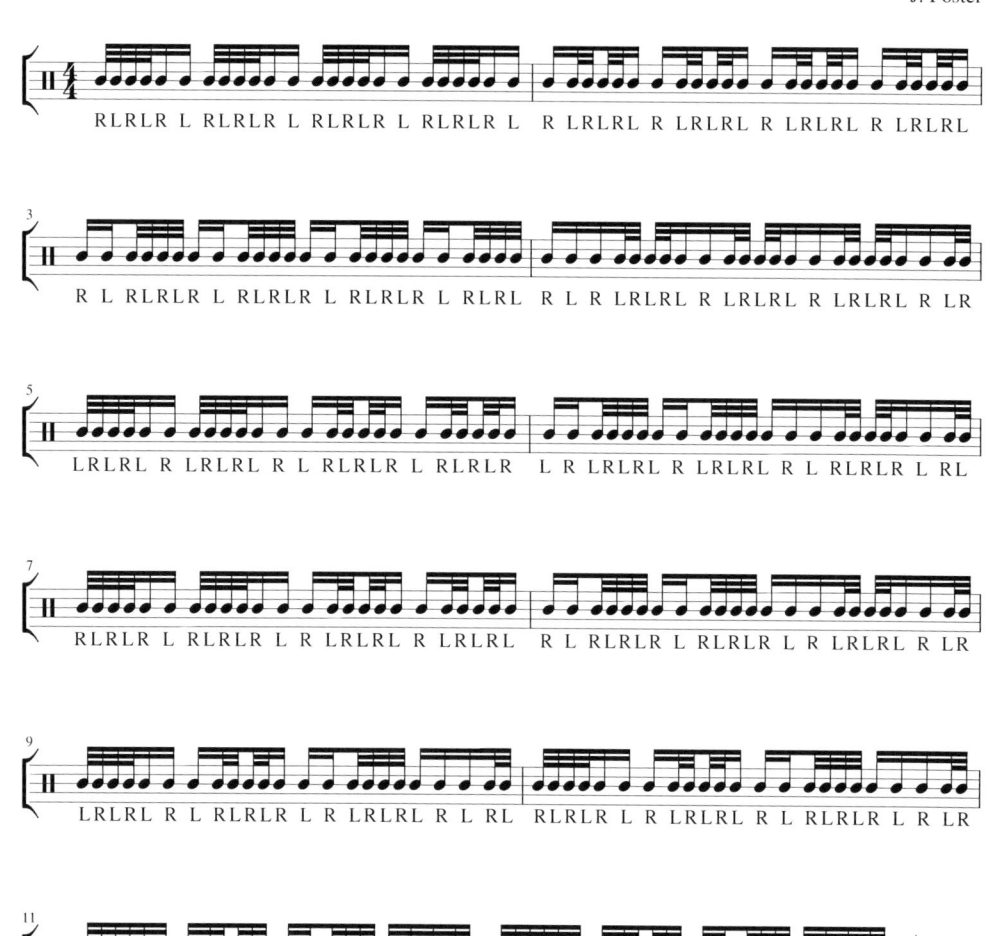

J. Foster

The Ultimate Burnout Blueprint (Spree)

J. Foster

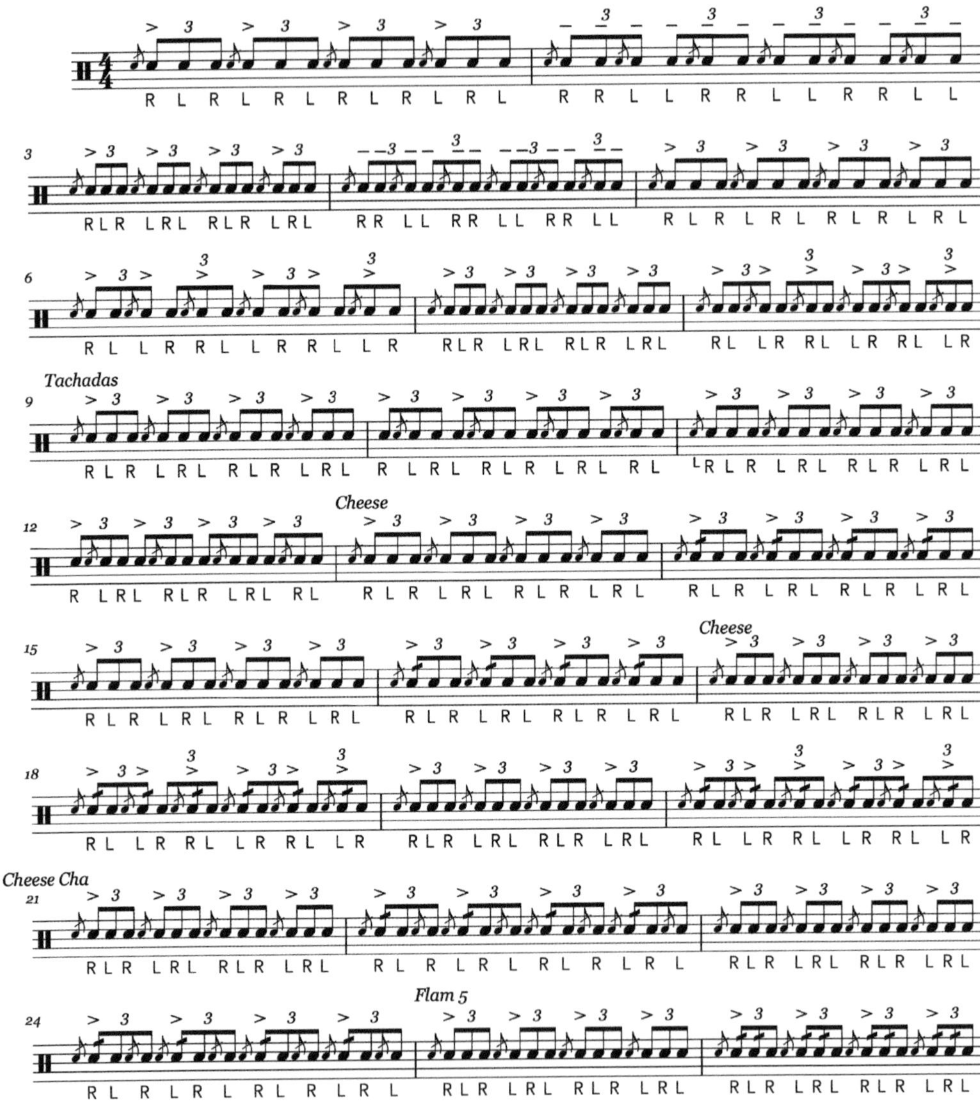

The Ultimate Burnout Blueprint (cont.)

GLOSSARY

A

Accent - Emphasis placed on a particular note that gives it more stress than the others.

Accent mark- The notation used to imply a note should be accented.

Attack - Sounds have a beginning, a middle, and an end. The initial sound spike is called the attack and is usually sharp and short-lived. Cymbals have a somewhat longer attack than drums.

B

Backstick/backsticking - A visually entertaining way of producing a note, using both ends of the stick by quickly flipping the stick from striking with the bead of the stick to striking with the butt of the stick.

Bar - The basic unit of music. One bar contains the full complement of the *time signature*.
See *measure*.

Bass drum - the lowest pitched drum in a marching band. It can be tuned to several toned pitches to add color to the lower rank of a percussion section.
See *tonal drum*.

Battery - The drum section of a marching band. It consists of snare drums, bass drums, tenor drums, and cymbals.

Bead - The small round, acorn- or barrel-shaped tip of a drum stick.

Beat - Basic unit of rhythm or pulse. For example, the *time signature* 4/4 specifies four quarter notes per *bar* or *measure*, which means four beats to a *bar* or *measure*.

Beats Per Minute (or BPM) - The standard method of specifying tempo. Metronomes are typically calibrated from 40 bpm to 208 bpm, although in practice, music tempos can be slower or significantly faster (the upper limit being around 400 bpm).

Bounce - The response of a drumstick/mallet after striking a drum. Some techniques require a certain amount of bounce to play cleanly and at speed.

Brushes - When a softer sound is required, a drummer might use brushes made of wire or plastic. Drum brushes resemble whisk brooms, which is what drummers used before wire brushes became available.

Buzz - A sound made by pressing the bead of a drum stick into the head and dragging it slightly. The technique causes the stick to bounce off the head several times, producing a buzzing sound.

Buzz Roll - A smooth, clean roll produced by *buzzing* the drumsticks onto the drum head.

C

Cadence - musical arrangement for percussionists that is usually played to maintain the correct rhythm in a drum corps or marching band.

Cheese - A double stroke preceded by a grace note. Often found in *hybrid rudiments*.

Chops - A term used to denote technique, usually about someone who has a lot of it coupled with remarkable speed in percussion.

Common Time - Another name for the 4/4 time signature. The signature is so dominant in all music forms that it is now considered the default signature. It is sometimes denoted by a large 'C' in the music staff.

Count - See *Beat, Time Signature*.

Crash - A sound produced by two cymbals colliding to add intensity to an ensemble's accent.

Crisp - Usually a reference to a *snare drum* that has a short, sharp, high-pitched *attack*.

Cross-Tuning - Tuning a drum by adjusting one tension bolt, then the bolt directly opposite, and proceeding around the drum. On an 8-lug drum, the pattern would be: 1, 5, 2, 6, 3, 7, 4, 8.

Cross-Stick - A striking technique of holding the drum stick bead against the drum head near the rim and striking the rim with the other end of the stick, producing a 'click' or 'clock' sound.

Cut Time - See *Half Time*.

Cymbal - a concave metal plate (as of brass or bronze) that produces a brilliant crashing tone and is struck with a drumstick or is used in pairs to be smashed together.

D

Diddle - a note consisting of two consecutively played strokes on one hand.

Diddle interpretation - refers to the clarity and cleanliness of a diddle.

Double paradiddle - One of the paradiddle-type rudiments in the 40 essential rudiments.
See *The 40 Essential Rudiments Blueprint* for details on how the double paradiddle is played and notated.

Double ratamacue - One of the drag-type rudiments in the 40 essential rudiments.
See *The 40 Essential Rudiments Blueprint* for details on how the double ratamacue is played and notated.

Down Stroke - the type of drum stroke where the stick height starts at a high height before striking the drum and ends at a low height after the drum is struck.

Dynamic strokes - a series of drum strokes that include *Full, Down, Tap,* and *Up* strokes.

Drag - One of the 40 essential rudiments.
See *The 40 Essential Rudiments Blueprint* for details on how the drag is played and notated.

Drag paradiddle #1, #2 - Two of the drag-type rudiments, incorporating both the paradiddle and drag rudiments into one complex rudiment.
See *The 40 Essential Rudiments Blueprint* for details on how the paradiddle is played and notated.

E

Eighth note - refers to a note that is 1/8th of the value of a quarter note. Eight notes are usually identified by their single beam or single tail/flag.

F

Flam - One of the 40 essential rudiments.
See *The 40 Essential Rudiments Blueprint* for details on how the flam is played and notated.
Flam tap - One of the flam rudiments in the 40 essential rudiments.
See *The 40 Essential Rudiments Blueprint* for details on how the flam tap is played and notated.

Flam accent - One of the flam-type rudiments in the 40 essential rudiments.
See *The 40 Essential Rudiments Blueprint* for details on how the flam accent is played and notated.

Flamacue - One of the flam type rudiments in the 40 essential rudiments.
See *The 40 Essential Rudiments Blueprint* for details on how the flamacue is played and notated.

Flam paradiddle - one of the 40 essential rudiments, combining two other rudiments: the flam and the paradiddle.
See *The 40 Essential Rudiments Blueprint* for details on how the flam paradiddle is played and notated.

Flam paradiddle-diddle - one of the 40 essential rudiments, combining two other rudiments: the flam and the paradiddle-diddle.
See *The 40 Essential Rudiments Blueprint* for details on how the flam paradiddle-diddle is played and notated.

Flam drag - One of the 40 essential rudiments.
See *The 40 Essential Rudiments Blueprint* for details on how the flam drag is played and notated.

Flat flam - The type of flam produced when both sticks hit the drumhead simultaneously, creating a flat sound.

Five stroke roll - One of the roll-type rudiments in the 40 essential rudiments.
See *The 40 Essential Rudiments Blueprint* for details on how the five-stroke roll is played and notated.

Fulcrum - refers to the point between the thumb and finger, where the drum stick is lightly gripped to maintain control.

Full stroke - the type of drum stroke where the stick height starts at a high height before striking the drum and ends at a high height after the drum is hit.

G

German grip- The technique of having either the right-hand parallel to the drumhead, used in the *traditional grip* or both hands, as used in the *matched grip*.

Ghost notes - Empty Notes that are played to mimic an actual playing stroke visually. Ghost notes are notated on percussion music in parenthesis.

Grace note - a note that is lightly felt and is played slightly before the dominant note.

Grip - the way a drumstick/mallet is held. There are two types of grips: *Traditional* and *matched grips*.

H

Half note - The type of note whose value is 1/2 a quarter note. Half notes are usually identified as a hollow dot with a stem attached.

Half time - Refers to a 4/4 measure that has been rhythmically cut to manipulate rhythm or tempo.

I

J

K

L

Lesson 25 - One of the drag-type rudiments. See *The 40 Essential Rudiments Blueprint* for details on how Lesson 25 is played and notated.

Legato stroke - See *full stroke*.

Lugs - Fittings attached to the drum's sides to hold the nut boxes and receivers in place.

M

Marching band - an ensemble of musicians whose purpose is to bring pride to a university or event.

Matched grip- the lesser form of grips used within drumline organizations, however widely popular within percussion ensembles and drum set performers, comprised of using *overhand grip* for both the right hand and left hand, causing both hands to be 'matched.'

Metronome - a device that measures the tempo (or speed) of music in BPM (beats per minute)

Measure - Commonly referred to as a *bar*.

N

Nine-stroke roll - One of the roll-type rudiments in the 40 essential rudiments.
See *The 40 Essential Rudiments Blueprint* for details on how the nine-stroke roll is played and notated.

O

open - to play in a way that the space between each note within a piece of music is much larger.

Overhand grip - the technique used by the right hand in the *traditional grip* or with both hands used in the *matched grip*.

P

Paradiddle - One of the 40 essential rudiments.
See *The 40 Essential Rudiments Blueprint* for details on how the paradiddle is played and notated.

Paradiddle-diddle - One of the paradiddle types of rudiments in the 40 essential rudiments. It involves adding an additional 'diddle' to the *paradiddle* rudiment.
See The 40 Essential Rudiments Blueprint for details on how the paradiddle-diddle is played and notated.

Pataflafla - One of the flam types of rudiments in the 40 essential rudiments.
See *The 40 Essential Rudiments Blueprint* for details on how the pataflafla is played and notated.

Percussion - The section of instruments in an ensemble whose instruments require striking a hand, stick, or mallet, including drums, cymbals, xylophone, piano, rattles, and gongs.

Practice pad - a pad whose surface can be made of various material types for percussion practice.

Primary note - The accented note of a flam, which comes directly after the flam's grace note is played.

Pulse - See *beat*.

Q

Quarter Note - The type of note whose value is 1/4th of a full measure. They can be identified as a filled dot with a stem.

R

Rebound - The natural response of the drumstick after striking the drumhead.

Rest - a period in music where a note is not to be played. They can be broken down as quarter rest, eighth rest, sixteenth rest, 32nd rest, etc.

Rim - a circular hoop piece used to hold the drum head and drum shell in place.

Rudiments - The building blocks of all percussion music. They are broken down into four types: Roll rudiments, paradiddle rudiments, flam rudiments, and drag rudiments.
See *The 40 Essential Rudiments Blueprint* for more details on how each rudiment is played and noted.

S

Seven stroke roll - One of the roll-type rudiments in the 40 essential rudiments. See The Rudiment Blueprint for details on how the paradiddle is played and notated.

Single Flammed mill - one of the flam type rudiments. See *The 40 Essential Rudiments Blueprint* for details on how the single flammed mill is played and notated.

Single ratamacue - One of the drag-type rudiments.
See *The 40 Essential Rudiments Blueprint* for details on how the single ratamacue is played and notated.

Single stroke four - One of the roll types of rudiments in the 40 essential rudiments.
See *The 40 Essential Rudiments Blueprint* for details on how the single stroke four is played and notated.

Single stroke roll - One of the 40 essential rudiments.
See *The 40 Essential Rudiments Blueprint* for details on how the paradiddle is played and notated.

Six stroke roll - One of the roll types of rudiments in the 40 essential rudiments.
See *The 40 Essential Rudiments Blueprint* for details on how the six-stroke roll is played and notated.

Single stroke seven - One of the roll types of rudiments. See *The 40 Essential Rudiments Blueprint* for details on how the single stroke seven is played and notated.

Stick - A device that is used to strike a percussion instrument.

T

Traditional grip - one of the more common forms of grips used by drumline organizations and percussion ensembles worldwide, comprised of having an underhand grip on the left hand and an overhand grip on the right hand.

Triple bounce roll - one of the roll types of rudiments. See *The 40 Essential Rudiments Blueprint* for details on how the triple bounce roll is played and notated.

Triple ratamacue - One of the 40 essential rudiments. See *The 40 Essential Rudiments Blueprint* for details on how the triple ratamacue is played and notated.

U

Underhand grip - the grip technique used by the left hand within the *traditional grip* method of holding drumsticks.

V

W

X

Y

z

About the Author

Jeremie Foster is a master in his craft. The notes he performs on the snare drum are so eloquently woven together that one would get chills from just the sound of his paradiddle. He's so masterful in his craft that this bio must be written in the third person.

Just kidding.

I am from BANKHEEEEAD, Atlanta, Georgia, A literal product of the hood, whose life was protected by God through the prayers of my loving mother. I picked up drumsticks at age three and never put them down. Something about drumming brings peace to me, no matter what I am going through. That's how I know this gift was blessed to me by God Himself.

I am an Alumnus of The Great Bethune-Cookman University with a Bachelor of Science in Computer Engineering. Now I know what you're thinking: why did I not major in music? Well, that's the thing: I love math and science just as much as I love music (but I love music a little more…don't judge me).

While at Bethune-Cookman University, I participated in the marching band (Let's Go Wildcats!), where I served as Head Section Leader of the percussion section, Sudden Impact Percussion, from 2014 to 2017 (S-S-S-S PHIIIII!).

Also, during my tenure at Bethune-Cookman University, I became a part of a few organizations that I hold dear to my heart to this day: Phi Mu Alpha Sinfonia Fraternity of America, Alpha Phi Alpha Fraternity, Inc., Snare Si Phi Fraternity Inc, and Mu Phi Sigma National Percussion Fraternity.

I am now working as a Software Developer for a Fortune500 Fintech company by day and a performer on the Atlanta Hawk's Drumline (ATL BOOM) by night. I am also the host of the podcast 'The Drum Lounge Podcast,' which is a podcast solely about drums and their influence and history in this nation.

As you can tell, I absolutely love drumming. Outside of my wife (Heyyyy Dreyah!), drumming is one of the main things I think about daily. I constantly thank God for my gift because I have no idea where I would be without it.

Before closing, I would like to end with a scripture that I live by when it comes to my love for percussion and teaching percussion to those who share the same passion:

"Each of you should use whatever gift you received to serve others, as faithful stewards of God's grace in its various forms."

1 Peter 4:10 (NIV)
QR codes directs readers to a page.

Printed in Great Britain
by Amazon